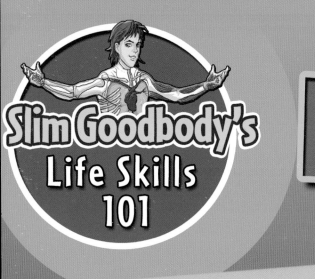

Slim Goodbody's Life Skills 101

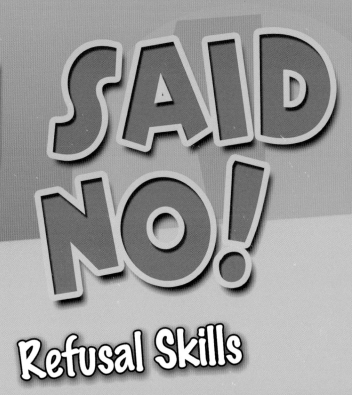

I SAID NO!

Refusal Skills

CRABTREE
Publishing Company
www.crabtreebooks.com

Crabtree Publishing Company
www.crabtreebooks.com

Series Development, Writing, and Packaging:
John Burstein, Slim Goodbody Corp.

Editors:
Reagan Miller, Valerie Weber, and Mark Sachner,
  Water Buffalo Books

Editorial director:
Kathy Middleton

Production coordinator:
Kenneth Wright

Prepress technicians:
Margaret Amy Salter, Kenneth Wright

Designer: Tammy West, Westgraphix LLC.

Photos: Chris Pinchback, Pinchback Photography

"Slim Goodbody" and Pinchback photos, copyright,
© Slim Goodbody

Photo credits:
iStockPhotos: p. 10
Shutterstock: p. 8 (top, left), 9 (all), 13 (top),
  14 (right), 15 (all), 22 (bottom)
© Slim Goodbody: p. 1, 4, 5, 6, 7, 11,, 12, 13 (bottom),
  14 (top, left), 16, 17 (all), 18 (all), 19, 20, 21 (all),
  22 (top), 23, 24, 25 (all), 26, 27, 28, 29.

Acknowledgements:
The author would like to thank the following
children for all their help in this project: Stephanie
Bartlett , Sarah Booth, Christine Burstein, Lucas
Burstein, Olivia Davis, Eleni Fernald, Kylie Fong,
Tristan Fong, Colby Hill, Carrie Laurita, Ginny
Laurita, Henry Laurita, Louis Laurita, Nathan
Levig, Havana Lyman, Renaissance Lyman,
Andrew McBride, Lulu McClure, Yanmei
McElhaney, Amanda Mirabile, Esme Power, Emily
Pratt, Andrew Smith, Dylan Smith, Mary Wells

"Slim Goodbody" and "Slim Goodbody's Life
Skills 101" are registered trademarks of the Slim
Goodbody Corp.

Library and Archives Canada Cataloguing in Publication

Burstein, John
    I said no! : refusal skills / John Burstein.

(Slim Goodbody's life skills 101)
Includes index.
ISBN 978-0-7787-4789-5 (bound).--ISBN 978-0-7787-4805-2 (pbk.)

    1. Peer pressure--Juvenile literature. 2. Decision making--Juvenile
literature. 3. Risk-taking (Psychology)--Juvenile literature. I. Title.
II. Title: Refusal skills. III. Series: Burstein, John. Slim Goodbody's
life skills 101.

HQ784.P43B87 2010   j303.3'27   C2009-903569-3

Library of Congress Cataloging-in-Publication Data

Burstein, John.
    I said no! : refusal skills / [John Burstein].
      p. cm. -- (Slim Goodbody's life skills 101)
    Includes index.
    ISBN 978-0-7787-4805-2 (pbk. : alk. paper) -- ISBN 978-0-7787-4789-5 (reinforced
library binding : alk. paper)
    1. Peer pressure in children--Juvenile literature. 2. Decision-making in children--
Juvenile literature. 3. Risk-taking (Psychology) in children--Juvenile literature. I.
Title. II. Series.

    HQ784.P43B87 2010
    305.23--dc22
                                              2009022850

Published in Canada
Crabtree Publishing
616 Welland Ave.
St. Catharines, Ontario
L2M 5V6

Published in the United States
Crabtree Publishing
PMB16A
350 Fifth Ave., Suite 3308
New York, NY 10118

Published in the United Kingdom
Crabtree Publishing
White Cross Mills
High Town, Lancaster
LA1 4XS

Published in Australia
Crabtree Publishing
386 Mt. Alexander Rd.
Ascot Vale (Melbourne)
VIC 3032

CONTENTS

Words in **bold** are defined
in the glossary on page 30.

CHOOSING REFUSING

Katie was shocked. Had she heard her friend correctly? STEAL!? Her best friend, Olivia, wanted her to steal a DVD from the movie store. Was Olivia completely crazy?

The two friends were at the mall. Katie's mom was at the store next door. She had given them **permission** to look for movies all by themselves.

"Come on," whispered Olivia. "Don't be such a chicken."

"I'm not a chicken," Katie hissed back. "I just think it's a dumb idea."

"No it's not. It's an adventure." Olivia's eyes were wide with excitement.

Katie didn't know what to do. Olivia wouldn't stop until she got her way.

"Everyone does it," said Olivia. "It's not a big deal."

"I don't think so," Katie said.

"I can't believe you are being this way." Olivia rolled her eyes at Katie.

"Stealing is wrong," Katie said. "Besides, my mom would never trust me again if she found out."

"Fine," said Olivia. "Then let's just borrow the DVD for a few days. We'll sneak it back the next time we come to the mall."

"We'll get caught," Katie said.

"Wait till I tell everyone what a little baby you are," Olivia added.

Katie felt sick inside. Olivia would make fun of her in front of all their friends if she said no.

What should she do?

Hi. My name is Slim Goodbody.

I understand that it's hard to say no to a friend, but there are times you have to do what's right. You don't want to lose your friend. But you also don't want to go along with something that you feel is wrong.

I wrote this book to help you learn how to say no and hopefully still keep your friends. There is a series of steps you can take called Refusal Skills. Practicing these skills will help you feel more confident saying "no."

Danger Ahead

As you grow older, you become more **responsible** for making decisions about what to say and do. Your parents or other adults won't always be around to decide for you. You will be faced with many new **situations**. Some of these situations can be dangerous.

WHY SAY "NO"?

Someone has probably already asked you to do something that you felt was wrong. It may have been risky or unhealthy. That is why learning Refusal Skills is so important. Saying "no" at the right time can help you

- stay healthier;
- keep safer;
- avoid trouble;
- feel better about yourself.

How Do You Know?

How do you know that something is wrong? There isn't one right answer for everyone. We're all different, so you must answer this question for yourself.

When Something Is Wrong

There may be a number of reasons that you feel something is wrong:

- It goes against the lessons your parents have taught you.
- It makes you feel afraid.
- It gives you a **queasy** feeling in your stomach.
- It goes against the rules at school.
- It feels unfair or unsafe.

Why Saying No Is Hard

Even when you have good reasons for saying "no," refusing can still be hard to do. One reason for this might seem a bit surprising.

Saying "no" is hard, because saying "yes" is a habit.

The habit of saying "yes" began when you were very young. For most people, it starts at about three years old. Before that age, though, saying "no" came much more easily.

THE TERRIBLE TWOS

When kids are between two and three years old, most go through a stage called "the terrible twos." During this stage, they start saying "no" a lot. Kids seem to want to do exactly the opposite of what their parents ask them to do. Here are some examples of conversations between kids going through the terrible twos and their parents.

Parent: "OK, honey, it's time to eat."
Kid: "No!"

Parent: "It's bath time."
Kid: "No!"

Parent: "We need to go. Hop in the car."
Kid: "No!"

Parent: "Please share your toy with your friend."
Kid: "No!"

The terrible twos is an important stage of growing up. It teaches kids that they have the power to make their own choices. But the choices they make can also create problems for them.

Parent Pleasers

Deep down inside, children want to please their parents and make them happy. When kids say "no," their parents often get upset. When their parents get upset, kids feel bad. As kids get a little older, they learn that saying "yes" makes their parents happier. The family gets along better. It makes sense to say "yes," and gradually it becomes a habit.

Refusing is Losing

Saying "yes" also becomes a habit in school. Think about it. What would happen if you started telling your teachers "no" when they asked you to do something? Would that cause problems? What would happen in basketball practice if you refused to do what your coach asked? No doubt about it, when it comes to school, "refusing is losing!"

Trouble Brewing

Year after year, at home and in school, you have learned the value of saying "yes." Doing what your parents and teachers ask of you makes life easier and more enjoyable. But there is possible trouble brewing!

PEERS APPEAR

As most kids grow older, they often spend more time with their peers. A peer is someone about your own age who does many of the things that you do. For example, your peers

- live in the same area you do;
- go to your school or one nearby;
- play many of the same sports that you do;
- enjoy the same books or music that you like;
- play many of the same video games that you enjoy;
- watch many of the same TV shows that you do.

Peers or Parents

As you spend more time with peers, their **opinions** become more important to you. There may come a time when you value your peers' opinions more than your parents' opinions. This can lead to problems. Your parents and teachers understand what's best for you. Your peers probably do not.

Peer Pressure

When you feel like you have to do what your friends are doing, it's called **peer pressure**. For example, imagine all your peers started wearing striped pajamas to school. Chances are good that soon you would be wearing striped pajamas as well. If everyone else starts doing something, it's natural for a person to think the group is right. That is peer pressure.

Giving in to peer pressure and wearing striped pajamas won't hurt you. Giving in to peer pressure and doing something dangerous is a totally different story.

HARD TO RESIST

You probably spend almost as much time with your peers as you do with your parents or **siblings**. Some of your peers may be close friends. Peers can become like a second family. Because you care about your peers, you want to please them. Peer pressure can be hard to resist. Even when you know something might be harmful, you could end up saying "yes" to it. You could go along with others instead of going your own way.

Here are some reasons you may give in to peer pressure:
- You want to be liked.
- You want to look cool.
- You don't want to let people down.
- You don't want anyone to be mad at you.
- You don't want anyone to make fun of you.
- You don't want to be left out.
- You're afraid of losing a friend.

Breaking the "Yes" Habit

When it comes to your peers, you need to break the "yes" habit. Stopping the habit does not mean you can't agree with most things. You just need to draw the line and say "no" when it comes to doing something

- that can hurt your body;
- that can make you feel bad about yourself;
- that can harm someone else;
- that can hurt someone's feelings;
- that can make you sick;
- that can make someone else sick;
- that is **illegal** or **dishonest**;
- that goes against what you believe;
- that can get you into trouble.

Be Brave

"No" may be only two letters long, but sometimes you need to be brave to say it. Saying "no" takes courage even when saying it is the right thing to do. Learning refusal skills will help. There are ten refusal skills in all.

CONSIDER THE CONSEQUENCES
(Refusal Skill One)

Before you agree to do something, consider the consequences. The word *consequence* means something that happens as a result of an action. For example:

- If you go to sleep really late, the consequence is that you'll probably feel tired the next day.

- If you don't eat for a day or two, the consequence is that you'll probably feel very hungry.

Big Deal

Sometimes the consequences of doing something are no big deal. Sometimes, however, they are very serious. At these times, saying "no" is very important. Here are some questions to ask as you consider the consequences of giving in to peer pressure:

- Would I feel bad about myself if I did it?
- Could anyone get hurt by what I'm being asked to do?
- Could I get hurt?
- Could I get into any kind of trouble?
- Could I get someone else into trouble?
- What kind of trouble could we get into?
- Would my parents or teachers be upset if I did this?

Think it Through

After thinking through the consequences, you'll have a much better understanding of what you should do. No one can do this thinking for you. You are responsible for your own choices. So make smart ones!

SAY "NO"
(Refusal Skill Two)

After thinking through the consequences, let's say you decide to say "no." It is now time to let others know your decision. Speak up in a firm, strong voice. Say "No" or "No, thanks."

If you start your sentence with "no," there can be no doubt about where you stand. When "no" is the first word out of your mouth, your peers will probably take you seriously.

Show You Mean It
(Refusal Skill Three)

When you say "no," be sure your **body language** shows you feel strongly about your decision. Body language is a way people **communicate** without using words. The way you hold your body says a lot about how you are feeling inside. If you want to show other people that you believe in what you are saying,

- shake your head from side to side as you say, "no";
- stand up straight;
- look them in the eye;
- keep a serious **expression** on your face.

If you're smiling, your peers might think you aren't serious. If you don't look them in the eye, you may seem unsure of yourself.

Practice Makes Perfect

It's a good idea to practice skills two and three at home in front of a mirror. Say "no" in a strong, clear voice. Check out your body language. Make sure you are standing in a way that looks strong and **confident**. Ask your parents or siblings to watch and listen.

SAY IT AGAIN
(Refusal Skill Four)

If your peers don't take "no" for an answer the first time, say it again. Keep repeating yourself. Sometimes it takes more than one "no" before others understand you mean what you say! Be firm and don't change your mind. You have a right to say "no" if something doesn't feel right to you.

Don't Apologize
(Refusal Skill Five)

When you say "no," you're not doing anything wrong. In fact, you are probably doing something right, so there is no reason to apologize. Do not offer an apology such as, "I'm sorry, but I have to say no." Saying you're sorry makes you sound less sure that you want to refuse. Your peers may think they can still wear you down and get you to do what they want.

Change the Channel
(Refusal Skill Six)

After you've said "no" one or more times, try to change the subject. Imagine you are changing the channel on the television. Switch to something your peers might find interesting. For example:

"Did you see the game last night on TV?"

"Did you study for the test tomorrow?"

"I am going to play soccer later tonight. Want to come, too?"

"I saw an amazing TV show last night."

"I just found out about an incredible video game!"

If you change the channel quickly enough, your peers might start thinking about what you've just said. They may stop asking you to do something you don't want to do.

Another way to change the subject is to say something funny. Sometimes humor is the best way to get people thinking about something else.

DON'T ASK WHY

(Refusal Skill Seven)

If your peers keep bugging you, don't ask them why they won't stop. If you do, it will just keep the discussion going. For example, suppose you say,

"Why do you keep bothering me when I've said no?"

This sounds **reasonable**, but it can easily lead to more pressure. The person might say,

"Because I think it's a good idea"

 or

"Because I know you really want to do it."

Then, you'll be right back where you started—saying "no." You might even get into a worse argument.

State Your Reason
(Refusal Skill Eight)

When your peers won't stop bugging you, move on to the next skill. Say exactly what you think is wrong with what you are being asked to do. Then, name the consequences. State your reason for saying no.

Your reason should be simple, clear, and honest. For example:

- "That's stealing, and stealing is wrong."
- "That's dangerous, and I could get really hurt."
- "That's mean, and I won't hurt somebody's feelings on purpose."
- "That's cheating, and I don't cheat."
- "That's breaking the rules, and I don't want to get into trouble."
- "That's against the law, and I don't want to be arrested!"
- "That's bad for me, and it could make me sick."

Don't be afraid to use your parents as an excuse. You could say:

- "My mom would be mad if I did that."
- "My mom wants me to come right home."

Once you give a reason for saying "no," your friends might stop bothering you.

OFFER OPTIONS

(Refusal Skill Nine)

You've said "no." You've tried to change the subject. You've given your reasons. If your friends are still pressuring you, here's what to do next. Suggest something you can all do instead. Think of an activity that will be fun or interesting.

Here are some examples of what you can say:

- "Let's go to my house instead."
- "Let's go for a bike ride instead."
- "Let's shoot some baskets instead."
- "Let's play catch instead."
- "Let's ask our parents if we can go to the movies instead."
- "Let's see if we can go to the mall instead."
- "Let's play a video game instead."

Make Your Exit
(Refusal Skill Ten)

Let's say your friends don't agree to do something different. Let's say they keep up the pressure. There is only one more step you can take. Your final step is to walk away. Leave the danger and the risk behind. You don't have to get mad or say something in anger. You can just say:

- "I think that's a really bad idea, so I'm going home."

- "I've got other things to do."

You can make your statement even simpler. It's perfectly OK just to say:

- "I'm leaving."

- "I'm out of here."

- "I'll see you guys tomorrow."

- "Good-bye."

KEEP THE DOOR OPEN

Even if you decide to leave, chances are that you still want to stay friends. If that is the case, let your friends know they are welcome to join you. For example, you might say:

- "I'm going to the park. If you change your mind, come on over."

- "If you decide to do something safer, give me a call."

- "I'll be at home if you want to come play video games."

- "I'm going for a bike ride. You can come, if you want."

By leaving in a friendly way, you are setting a positive example. Don't be surprised if your friends take you up on your offer.

Follow the Leader

It's not easy to resist peer pressure, especially when everyone seems to be following along.

You need to really trust in yourself and in your own judgment.

Going Your Own Way

If you choose to turn in your own direction, you will probably feel much better about yourself. You may even have a positive **influence** on some other peers. They might be feeling the same way that you are, but they don't know how to say "no." When people are unsure of what to do, they often look to others to set an example. When you speak out, you may give some of your peers the courage to also say no.

REFUSAL SKILL REVIEW

You've learned ten refusal skills. That's a lot. Here is a list to help you remember all of them. Review these skills and think about how you can use them in a difficult situation.

One: Consider the Consequences
Two: Say "No"
Three: Show You Mean It
Four: Say It Again
Five: Don't Apologize
Six: Change the Channel
Seven: Don't Ask Why
Eight: State Your Reason
Nine: Offer Options
Ten: Make Your Exit

It may sound a bit strange at first, but sometimes you need to say "no" to yourself! Sometimes you may feel a bit of a split inside. One part of you wants to do something that another part of you doesn't think is such a good idea. You are feeling self pressure.

Saying No To Yourself

Of course, you're really only one person, but sometimes you can hold two opinions at the same time. For example, suppose you have a test coming up tomorrow. One part of you knows that you need to study. Another part just wants to play and have fun. When that happens, you can use some of the refusal skills that you've learned to help you make a good choice.

Begin with Skill One and consider the consequences.

Ask yourself,

"If I don't study, how well am I likely to do on the test?"

If you decide that you won't do very well, go on to Skill Two.

Tell yourself,

"No, I can't play."

Jump to Skill Eight and give a reason.

You can tell yourself,

"If I don't study, I can fail the test. If I fail the test, I will feel really bad about myself."

You can even use Skill Nine and give yourself an option.

You can tell yourself,

"Instead of playing now, I'll play after I study."

BE PREPARED

You never know if and when you'll be asked to do something that you think is wrong. You'll be taken by surprise, so it is best to be prepared ahead of time. Figure out ahead of time what you believe in. You will then be able to say "yes" or "no" with confidence. Nobody can decide for you. You must look inside your own heart and mind to discover your true feelings.

Tough Questions

Here are some questions you can ask yourself. Some of them may be tough to answer. Be sure you take the time to really think them through and answer them as fully and truthfully as you can. Write down your answers so you can review them at a later time.

- How important is honesty to me?
- Why is honesty important?
- How important is being liked?
- Would I do anything to be liked?
- How important is being respected?
- What kind of person deserves respect?
- How far will I go to keep a friend?
- Would I make someone cry on purpose?
- How much danger am I willing to put myself or others in?
- Would I do something to risk my health?
- Do I want to be a good person?
- What are the qualities that make a person good?
- What would make me do something I didn't want to do?

Now You Know

Knowing what you value and believe in will help you decide what to do in difficult situations. You also now have a powerful set of refusal skills to help you. Use them with confidence. Remember, saying "yes" or "no" is up to you. The next time you feel peer pressure or self pressure, choose wisely.

GLOSSARY

body language The way a person moves or holds himself or herself that communicates to other people

communicate To give information, thoughts, or feelings to other people

confident Sure of oneself and one's actions

dishonest Not honest, unfair

expression The look on someone's face that communicates a feeling, thought, or emotion

illegal Against the law

influence Effect on someone

opinions A person's belief in or thoughts about something

option A choice; the power or right to choose

peer pressure Refers to people of the same age or group encouraging or putting pressure on others to change their beliefs or actions

permission Refers to agreeing to let someone do something

queasy Sick; Often a feeling in the stomach that comes from being nervous about something

reasonable Showing good sense; not silly or unfair

responsible Refers to having something as a concern or duty

siblings Brothers or sisters

situations The way things are; conditions

FOR MORE INFORMATION

BOOKS

How to Say No and Keep Your Friends: Peer Pressure Reversal for Teens and Preteens. Sharon Scott. HRD Press.

PeerPressure: Deal with it without losing your cool. Elaine Slavens (Author), Ben Shannon (Illustrator). Lorimer.

Stick Up for Yourself: Every Kid's Guide to Personal Power & Positive Self-Esteem. Gershen Kaufman (Author), Lev Raphael (Author), Pamela Espeland (Author). Free Spirit Publishing.

Hot Issues, Cool Choices: Facing Bullies, Peer Pressure, Popularity, and Put-downs. Sandra McLeod Humphrey (Author), Brian Strassburg (Illustrator). Prometheus Books.

WEB SITES

The Cool Spot
www.thecoolspot.gov/pressures.asp
Watch videos, play games, and learn a lot about risky behavior, peer pressure, and how to make good choices.

Kidshealth
kidshealth.org/kid/feeling/friend/peer_pressure.html
Check out this Web site for information on how to deal with peer pressure.

Kids' Health: Child and Youth Health
www.cyh.com/HealthTopics/HealthTopicDetailsKids.aspx?p=335&np=286&id=1822
Visit this Web site to learn about making good choices and resisting peer pressure. You can also play games and read what other kids have to say about staying healthy.

Slim Goodbody
www.slimgoodbody.com
Discover loads of fun and free downloads for kids, teachers, and parents.

INDEX

About the Author
John Burstein (also known as Slim Goodbody) has been entertaining and educating children for over thirty years. His programs have been broadcast on CBS, PBS, Nickelodeon, USA, and Discovery. He has won numerous awards including the Parent's Choice Award and the President's Council's Fitness Leader Award. Currently, Mr. Burstein tours the country with his multimedia live show "Bodyology." For more information, please visit **slimgoodbody.com**.

Printed in the USA—CG